JACKSON HELENS

JOB SEARCH GUIDE

The Essential Guide On How to Land A Perfect Job,
Learn Everything From Finding Jobs to Effective Interview Hints and
Techniques That Will Help You Land Your Dream Job

Descrierea CIP a Bibliotecii Naționale a României
JACKSON HELENS
    JOB SEARCH GUIDE. The Essential Guide On How to
Land A Perfect Job, Learn Everything From Finding Jobs to
Effective Interview Hints and Techniques That Will Help You
Land Your Dream Job / Jackson Helens. – Bucharest: Editura My
Ebook, 2020
    ISBN 978-606-983-609-5

JACKSON HELENS

JOB SEARCH GUIDE

The Essential Guide On How to Land A Perfect Job,
Learn Everything From Finding Jobs to Effective
Interview Hints and Techniques
That Will Help You Land Your Dream Job

My Ebook Publishing House
Bucharest, 2020

TABLE OF CONTENTS

INTRODUCTION

When you sit down to interview with a prospective employer that you are sincerely interested in working for, there are probably more than a hundred different things running through your mind at one time, which can make you anxious and cause you to walk into the interview unprepared. However, if you can focus yourself on the most important facets of the employment interview, then you will be able to relax yourself better and to be more in control of the message that you are sending to the prospective employer.

Many people find it helpful to know exactly what they should not do in the interview, as this helps people develop a good idea of what they should do in the interview. Job interview mistakes can easily be avoided, and many of the same mistakes cause a large number of the job force to fail in their job interviews on a consistent basis. By avoiding these truly lethal job interview mistakes, you will be able to show prospective

7

employers that you are the right candidate for the job that you are applying for.

There are ten critical mistakes that people make during their job interviews. By avoiding these ten critical mistakes, you can launch yourself forward, proving that you are the right candidate for the job rather than making a fatal mistake that will cost you the job of your dreams.

The ten most critical mistakes to avoid in your initial job interview are as follows

Critical Mistake 01 - Inadequate Preparation for the Interview # Critical Mistake 02 - Arriving Too Early or Too Late

Critical Mistake 03 - Having the Wrong Attitude

Critical Mistake 04 - Being Unprepared for Interview Questions

Critical Mistake 05 - Not Asking the Right Questions

Critical Mistake 06 - Dressing Inappropriately

Critical Mistake 07 - Asking about Salary or Benefits

Critical Mistake 08 - Not Arriving with the Right Documents

Critical Mistake 09 - Being Dishonest or Impolite

Critical Mistake 10 - Marketing Yourself Incorrectly

Critical Job Interview Mistake 01 - Inadequate Preparation for the Interview

One of the most critical mistakes that you can make in a job interview is to arrive unprepared for the interview. There are too many job seekers out there who do not do any research into the company that they are interviewing for. How can you prove that you are the right candidate for a job or a specific position if you do not know anything about the job for which you are applying?

Benjamin Franklin is known for a famous quote, "By failing to prepare you are preparing to fail", and this quote is never more applicable than when it comes to preparing for a job interview. It is imperative that you do all of the necessary homework long beforehand. If you come off as an enthusiastic and committed candidate for the job, you will have a much better chance of impressing whoever is interviewing you.

As soon as you find out that you will be interviewing for a company, research them and the position that you will be interviewing for. This way, you can demonstrate that you are absolutely the right candidate for the job by answering the questions that your interviewer poses effectively and intelligently. You will also be able to prepare the most appropriate questions to ask of your interviewer as well.

The most obvious way to prepare yourself for a job interview is to visit the website for the company that you are interviewing with. You will find a lot of useful information on most company websites. Other website resources that are worth exploring include websites relating to the industry, websites offering business information, and websites belonging to competing companies. You may also want to visit your local library to find out about relevant periodicals and directories.

Another useful idea is to visit the company beforehand, picking up any relevant information and brochures that are available there. You may also feel inclined to observe for a little while. The better prepared that you are for your interview ahead of time, the greater your chances will be for success.

You will find that many of the principals in this report tie in together. For example, preparing yourself for your job interview will have a great impact on avoiding a number of the critical mistakes that follow after this one. For example, by researching the employer and company beforehand, you can

12

better prepare yourself both to answer questions posed by the interviewer, and to ask the right questions when prompted. Preparing yourself with the right information about the company beforehand can have a significant impact on how comfortable and prepared you come across to the employer. This is one of the most ideal ways to prove that you are the right candidate for the job.

Critical Job Interview Mistake 02 - Arriving Too Early or Too Late

One of the most common mistakes that job seekers make going in to an interview, one that can easily compromise an entire interview is arriving at the wrong time. It is difficult to overcome this initial bad impression created either by arriving too late for the appointment, or by arriving far too early and forcing the interviewer to change their schedule in order to accommodate you. Luckily, there are a couple of different techniques that you can employ in order to avoid making this seriously costly mistake.

It is imperative that you arrive on time to your job interview appointment. You do not necessarily have to arrive at the appointment time on the dot, but a few minutes early is actually preferable. Make sure that you have working directions, which may mean driving them to test the travel time before the actual day of the interview. You may want to make a complete practice run to make sure that you have the timing right. Make sure that your dry run is completed at the same time as your interview, so you can gauge the traffic at that time during the day.

Make sure that you have all of the information that you need long beforehand so that you are not scrambling at the last minute in preparation. For example, you should write down the name of the person that you are supposed to ask for, so that you can go directly to the right place once you arrive. You should also make sure to bring all of the necessary documentation, which we will touch on later on in this report - But the important consideration to make is that you should gather all of your necessary documentation long beforehand so that you are not scrambling at the last minute to print out resumes, or to gather references and work samples to bring with you.

Arriving in a flustered rush is not a good way to show up to your interview. The whole intention of a job interview is to prove that you are the right candidate for a job, and if you prove your unreliability the first day that you meet the interviewer, you will have difficulty proving otherwise.

Being too early for your initial job interview can be just as critical a mistake as arriving late. If you arrive an hour early or more, you may be forcing the interviewer to change their schedule in order to accommodate you, and that is not a good way to get the interview started. If you want to impress the interviewer by being prompt, aim for 10 to 15 minutes early rather than a whole hour or more. By arriving fifteen minutes early, you have ample time to let the interviewer be notified of your arrival without forcing them to accommodate you long before the interview is set to begin.

When it comes to arriving at your job interview, the best thing that you can do is arrive either right on time, or with ten or fifteen minutes to spare. Arriving late is essentially asking to be dismissed. People who have turned up late for job interviews have literally been turned away, because employers are not looking for people who cannot prove their own selves to be dependable and trustworthy from day one.

Your interview is your first impression to your prospective employer, and your main intention should be to impress future employers in as many ways as you can.

Critical Job Interview Mistake 03 - Having the Wrong Attitude

There are a number of different behaviors during an interview that can cause you to come across as a negative person, or simply a person who does not have the right positive attitude for the job in question.

Coming across as a negative person can be the result of a wide variety of different behaviors that occur during the interviewing process. For example, if you should happen to make complaint regarding previous jobs, positions, bosses, co workers, colleagues or companies can send a rather negative message to your prospective employer, and should be avoided at all costs.

Something else that can create a negative impression is inappropriate body language. The following body language actions can all offer a negative message to the person who is interviewing you -

- Hunching down
- Slumping in the chair
- Avoiding eye contact with the interviewer
- Looking down constantly
- Folding your arms over your chest
- Fiddling with your hair
- Fiddling with items on the desk

There are also a number of verbal and non-verbal signals that give off a negative attitude to the person who is interviewing you, including but not limited to -

- speaking inaudibly
- speaking quietly
- mumbling
- the use of words like 'like' or 'um' repeatedly

It is important that you practice your answers to test interview questions, and your questions about the company in front of a mirror in order to improve the tone of your voice and your positive body language. By practicing beforehand, you can eliminate flaws in your interview demeanor which can give you a better chance of being successful in your interview.

Critical Job Interview Mistake 04 - Being Unprepared for Interview Questions

There are two important elements to a job interview - The first is the questions that the interviewer asks of you, and the second is the questions that you ask of the interviewer in return. If you are unable to properly articulate the right answers to the interview questions that are asked of you, you will most certainly have difficulty conveying the fact that you are the ideal candidate for the position to the person who is interviewing you.

The best way for you to avoid this practice is to think about your answers and to prepare them beforehand. There are many resources for common job interview questions, and most employers within different industries ask the same questions or at least similar sets of relevant questions which means that you can be prepared to a certain degree no matter what job you are applying for.

Prepare your answers to the most common job interview questions within your industry long before your interview. What questions are most likely going to be asked during the interview? What is normally required of a successful candidate for the position that you are applying for? There are a number of basic or general questions that tend to crop up in almost all job interviews, including but not limited to the following questions -

- What are your strengths, or what is your greatest strength?

- What are your weaknesses, or what is your greatest weakness?

- Why do you want this job position?

- What are some of your achievements to date? What has been your greatest achievement in your working history?

- Why are you the ideal candidate for this position? Why should we employ you rather than another candidate?

- If we were to call up your former employer or employers, what would they say about you?

Prepare and practice the answers to questions like these, and you will be able to avoid this critical initial job interview mistake. You do not want to suddenly go blank during the interview process, and this can easily be avoided simply by preparing beforehand and figuring out the most effective answers in order to appear both confidant and poised to the employer who is interviewing you.

Critical Job Interview Mistake 05 - Not Asking the Right Questions

There are two important elements to a job interview - The first is the questions that the interviewer asks of you, and the second is the questions that you ask of the interviewer in return. At some point during the job interview, the person interviewing you is going to ask "Do you have any questions for me?" And this is a question that makes a lot of people tremble. Failing to ask the right, most appropriate questions simply shows a lack of interest and forethought. As a result, this is one of the most critical mistakes that a job interview candidate can make.

Use the company research that you conducted earlier based on Critical Job Interview Mistake number 01, and prepare questions about the company that are insightful as the best and most efficient way to impress the interviewer you are working with. This will also help you gain the information that you need in order to make the most well informed job decision possible.

22

During your job interview, you should not sit like a bump on a log. Instead, you should make a real effort to show interest in the company, which can easily be done by asking the employer excellent interview questions in return. This shows the interviewer that you are interested in the company and that you have done your research and arrived prepared. Here are some of the questions that you may want to ask your interviewer. Keep in mind that when asked "Do you have any questions for me?", "Hmm, nope" is NOT a good answer.

- What are your biggest challenges?
- What is the average day like for this particular position?
- What specific tasks will be expected of me in this position?
- What is the next step following the interview?
- Is this a newly created job position or am I replacing another employee?
- How will my job performance be measured?
- What are the immediate goals of the department that I will be working in?
- What is the biggest challenge that the company is currently facing?

- What competitive advantages does the company have over other similar companies?

- What does the interviewer like best about the company?

- What could I do within this role that would make your job (The employer's job) easier?

- Is there anything else that I can further clarify for you?

- How do I compare with other candidates that have already been interviewed?

Critical Job Interview Mistake 06 - Dressing Inappropriately

Another critical mistake that many people make when it comes to initial job interviews should not come as a surprise: Dressing inappropriately. While most people seeking jobs know that dressing appropriately is a big part of arriving prepared to a job interview, most people do not actually have a good understanding of what "dressing appropriately" actually means. As a result, many people arrive at their interview dressed inappropriately, either in general or based on the dress code in question.

As it was mentioned before, it is important to research the company that you are interviewing with before hand. This comes in handy for a number of different reasons, one of which is so that you can dress according to the dress code that the rest of the employees are abiding by. By visiting the company before hand and doing a little bit of observing, you can figure out what style of dress would be ideal.

Get to know the culture of the company. If the company's employees are all wearing conservative clothing, then business casual is not going to cut it when you arrive at your interview. If you want to look like you already belong with the company, which should be your aim to begin with, then it is important that you dress not only to impress, but also to fit in at the same time.

You also need to avoid appearances that are excessive, extreme, bright or loud. Resist the temptation to wear colors that are bright, perfumes or body mists that are strong in smell, loud nail polish, or extravagant jewelry. If you have tattoos, cover them up. If you have piercings that are inappropriate, such as earrings for men, or anything other than earrings for women, take the jewelry out or cover the piercings with a band aid.

It is important that your interviewer focuses on your skills, your accomplishments and the real reasons for why you are the best candidate for the job, rather than your appearance. If your appearance fits in with the dress and appearance of the other employees in the company, your interviewer will be able to focus on your strengths rather than your loud appearance or the fact that your dress does not fit in with the company.

Critical Job Interview Mistake 07 - Asking about Salary or Benefits

While we have already touched on asking the right questions, we did not really focus on refraining from asking the WRONG ones. One of the biggest initial job interview mistakes that you can make is to ask about salary or benefits during your interview. The appropriate time for you to discuss compensation and benefit information is once a real, firm offer has been placed on the table. You should refrain from bringing this topic up prematurely.

Take the time to learn more about the company and the position that the company is looking to fill. In the end, money is not everything, and is definitely not what you should be obsessing about before you have even fully proven yourself to the company that you are interviewing with. Career satisfaction comes in a variety of different forms, so focus on joining a collaborative team environment with plenty of opportunity for growth rather than worrying about the benefits package. During the interview process, you should focus and concentrate on the things that really matter - Not compensation.

There are a number of other questions that should be avoided during the initial job interviewing process. The following is a list of questions in addition to "What is my salary?" that you should avoid at all costs when interviewing with a potential employer.

- How long does it take to be promoted? - While it may be fruitful to ask about advancement within the company, it is more important that you focus on the job that you are actually interviewing for.

- When will I be able to take a vacation? - If you are already asking this question at the interview, then you are already thinking about taking time off, and this does not look good to the employer.

- Will I be required to work overtime? - Asking about the hours that you will work says that you are the type of person who likes to watch the clock, and this is not something that a hiring manager is going to want to look for.

- What kinds of employee activities are held? - This question can be a real interview killer. It tells the interviewer that you are more interested in the company activities than in working hard and moving up within the company. Wait until you are hired before you begin to ask questions like this.

- What can I use my company computer for? Even though many employees use their computers for purposes other than for company work, you should never bring this up during an interview. This shows both a lack of maturity, and a lack of business sense as well.

- Will I be able to work from home? - While this may appear to be a good question, new employees need to come to understand the dynamics and the politics of the office before they should even begin to think about working at home. New employees cannot learn anything about the tempo, the faces, the politics and the dynamics of the company if they are working at home. The hiring manager is going to be looking for someone who will be right there all the time, both working and soaking up the dynamics of the office in order to become more successful and to make the company more successful as well.

- While many of these questions may seem naïve, and when you see them in print you may wonder why anyone would ever think to ask them, all of these questions have been asked through numerous job interviews in the past. So there are people out there who are naïve enough to ask these questions in job interviews - And many of them do not understand why they did not land the job after the fact.

Not only is it important to know what questions not to ask, it is also important to have a small list of questions that you SHOULD ask, so that you can be prepared when the person interviewing you asks "Is there anything that you want to ask me?" The only thing worse than asking an interview killer of a question, is simply saying "No".

Critical Job Interview Mistake 08 - Not Arriving with the Right Documents

Just because you were called in for an interview, it simply does not mean that your prospective employer has a copy of your resume or curriculum vitae on hand. Many employers conduct group interviews, so they may not necessarily be prepared to work with you by keeping your documents handy. It would be a large and critical mistake for you to arrive to your job interview without the documents that you need.

Make sure that you bring several copies of your resume so that everyone who attends the interview can have a copy and so that copies can be passed around as needed. Not only will this help you prepare yourself and your interviewers for the interview, but it will also show the person or people interviewing you that you had the consideration and foresight to come into the interview room prepared.

Make sure that you have a portfolio put together if your job interview requires it. Make sure that you have copies of any and all necessary documentation, including your resume, your curriculum vitae, recommendations, references, work samples, and anything else that is required in order to prove your work as a candidate for the job that you are applying for.

Before your interview, it is important that you have the right documents prepared. This should include directions to the interview site, and you should make sure you have enough time not only to get there, but also to find a parking space depending on the driving directions. Make sure that you are leaving early so that you can arrive between ten and fifteen minutes. Make sure that you have extra copies of your resume, along with a list of references both personal and professional, a notepad so that you can take notes, a daily planner, and a pen and a pencil so that you can take notes and make other important notations during your interview.

You may be able to enhance your professional look by carrying a portfolio, a folder or a briefcase. You should also make sure to know the details, such as the name and the title of the person you are supposed to meet with. You should also have conducted research on the company that you are applying for.

If you have taken notes on the research of the company, you may want to bring them and continue adding to them as you interview, but only as long as you are willing to let the interviewer see what notes you have already taken. This is a testament to what information you find most important in your job search.

Prepare for the toughest questions so that you will not have to pause when asked important things, such as "Where do you see yourself in 5 to 10 years?"

Having the right paperwork and documents prepared is the best way to arrive at an interview. Arriving on time, with your resume or curriculum vitae in hand, and work samples or other information as needed is a great way to show your prospective employer not only that you are taking this job interview seriously, but also that you are hardworking and dependable, and that you know how to make a good impression on the people who really matter within the company.

The more prepared you are, the more successful you will be.

Critical Job Interview Mistake 09 - Being Dishonest or Impolite

Your overall attitude has a lot to do with how your prospective employers perceive you and your candidacy for the position they are hiring for. There are a couple of things that you can do to make sure that your prospective employer or interview you sees you in the right light and does not get the wrong idea. Here are two things that you absolutely need to keep in mind -

Dishonesty - You should never, ever lie to an employer under any circumstances to get the position that you want. By lying or being dishonest in general, you are greatly undermining your own abilities and strengths, and you are destroying any trust or rapport that has been developed by the interviewer.

If you are unable to get the position that you want based on your current skills or potential skills and accomplishments, then you probably should not be applying for that particular position anyway. Applying for a position that is beyond your capabilities is simply asking for trouble. Being dishonest about your capabilities to get a job that is beyond your means is an even greater and more dangerous risk.

Being Impolite - you need to keep in mind that the person who is interviewing you may very well be your future boss or employer. You should not sit down until you are asked to. If you want to take off your jacket, you should ask for permission first. If refreshments are offered, thank your host.

You should make a point to express your interest toward the job or position that you are interested in applying for, and you should also make a point to thank the person interviewing you for the time that they took to sit and speak with you.

Even if you are no longer interested in the job that you are applying for by the end of your interview, the person who you sat down and spoke with may still be an excellent contact person with you.

You should absolutely never ever burn any bridges with potential employers or other people working within your industry of choice because there is no telling whether or not they will be helpful for you in the future. If you managed to obtain a job interview through an agency, you should also give them a phone call promptly following your interview so that you can advise them of whether or not you are interested in the role that you are interviewing for.

A large part of your interview success will hinge on your attitude, your willingness to listen, your willingness to ask and answer questions, and your ability to be honest and to have a positive outlook on the interview situation. If you are not projecting the right attitude and appearance to your prospective employer, you will have great difficulty when it comes to proving that you are the right candidate for the job, especially when there is a lot of competition for the job in question.

Critical Job Interview Mistake 10 - Marketing Yourself Incorrectly

This is another vital and critical mistake that needs to be avoided in your initial job interview. It is imperative that you market yourself correctly in your job interview in order to be successful when proving yourself as the ideal candidate for a specific company or position.

You need to be able to define yourself properly, and to map out your skills to the skills that the job you are applying for requires. You need to know what your major strengths are, and your major accomplishes, especially as they relate to the job that you are hoping to apply and interview for. You need to use the questions you ask and the answers to the questions the interviewer asks to make you really stand out.

Your goal should be to become memorable in the eyes of your future employer without standing out in a negative way. If you have unusual job experiences, interesting skills, unusual hobbies or other characteristics that will help you stand out from the other candidates applying for the job, then you should bring this up in a way that is natural. Now should not be the time to name drop, and you should not be aiming to make the interviewer feel uncomfortable or inadequate in any way.

Conclusion

When you finally do sit down to interview with a prospective employer and you are really, sincerely interested in working for them, then it is important for you to be prepared to handle every facet of the job interview. If you can focus yourself on the most important facets of the initial employment interview with a company that you are serious about working for, then you should be able to relax yourself, as well as to be more in control of the message that you are trying to send to the prospective employer.

By now you should have a pretty basic idea of the biggest and most critical mistakes that need to be avoided in your initial job interview if you want to be successful in proving to the interviewer that you are the best candidate for the job. There is an art to job interviews, and by taking the tips and information in this report seriously, you have already taken positive steps to mastering this excellent art. Once you learn how to master job interviews, you will not have trouble securing any job or position that you want.

By avoiding these ten critical mistakes, you can launch yourself forward, proving that you are the right candidate for the job rather than making a fatal mistake that will cost you the job of your dreams.

It may be surprising how easily a handful of small mistakes could affect your job interview success in some pretty serious ways. If you are serious about the job that you are applying for, and you really want to stand out as a positive and memorable candidate, then it is absolutely vital that you avoid these ten critical mistakes.

Now that you know how to avoid making these critical mistakes in your initial job interview - Let us go over a recap of what we have talked about in this report. There are ten critical mistakes that need to be avoided if you want to be successful in the job interview process.

Critical Mistake 01 - Inadequate Preparation for the Interview - Show up to your interview with the right preparation. Research the company and the job that you are applying for long before you leave for your interview.

Critical Mistake 02 - Arriving Too Early or Too Late - The best way to arrive to your interview is to show up ten to fifteen minutes early. Arriving too early or too late can seriously hurt your chances of job interview success.

Critical Mistake 03 - Having the Wrong Attitude - Your attitude says a lot about how serious you are about the job and the job interview. Have the right attitude and avoid verbal and non-verbal cues that you are distracted or that your heart is not truly in the interview.

Critical Mistake 04 - Being Unprepared for Interview Questions - Most interviewers ask very similar questions which means that you can prepare yourself a great deal before you walk in to your interview. Practice your answers to the tougher interview questions and you will have better luck answering them in the interview.

Critical Mistake 05 - Not Asking the Right Questions - At the end of most interviews, the person who is interviewing you will ask "Do you have any questions for me?" You need to be prepared to ask questions that are relevant to the job in question.

Critical Mistake 06 - Dressing Inappropriately - While most people think they have a good idea of what interview dress is like, many are wrong. It would be advisable for you to scope out the work place beforehand so that you can dress appropriately before you arrive.

Critical Mistake 07 - Asking about Salary or Benefits - There are a number of questions that you should absolutely refuse to bring up during the interview process, one of which relates to salary and benefits which should not be brought up until a job offer is on the table.

Critical Mistake 08 - Not Arriving with the Right Documents - Preparing yourself with the right documents, including work samples, references, referrals, recommendations and copies of your curriculum vitae or resume is vital to being ready for an interview and showing your interviewer that you are serious about the job.

Critical Mistake 09 - Being Dishonest or Impolite - Attitude is everything. Be honest, be polite, and give your prospective employer a good impression of who you are. After all, your interviewer may very well be your future boss!

Critical Mistake 10 - Marketing Yourself Incorrectly - Job interviews are all about marketing yourself right. Sell your skills, talents and hobbies and make yourself memorable and you will go far. The more memorable you are, the more you will stand out from other candidates who are trying to get the same job that you are interested in. Stand out from the crowd in your interview, and you truly will go far.

- You truly are on your way to mastering the art of the successful job interview! The more you practice in front of a mirror, the more you will be able to fine tune your ability to answer questions properly, to ask questions well, to eliminate negative habits or negative attitudes, and to create an appearance that is visually appealing to your prospective employer while giving them the impression that you are an excellent candidate for whatever job you are applying for.

By avoiding these ten critical mistakes in your initial job interview, you will have much greater success in your interviews, it's that simple. Good luck!

9 786069 836354

Printed by Libri Plureos GmbH in Hamburg, Germany